NEW DAY

HELEN STEINER RICE

TINY TREASURE-SERIES

Fleming H. Revell

FOR EACH NEW DAY

ISBN 0-8007-7143-5

Whenever you are troubled,
Put your problems in
God's hand,
For He has faced all problems
And He will understand.

Trouble and anguish have come
upon me, but thy commandments
are my delight.
Psalm 119:143

Today do not be concerned
about outward appearances;
rather concentrate on the
necessity and importance of
inner beauty.

When your day
is pressure-packed
And your hours are all too few,
Just close your
eyes and meditate
And let God talk to you.

*May my meditation be pleasing
to him, as I rejoice in the Lord.*

Psalm 104:34 NIV

Today, if God delays in
answering your prayer, continue
to keep the faith, knowing that
God has His own timetable.

Jana we
wish you all
a Merry Xmas.
Please use this
money for all of
you equally
or for Necessities

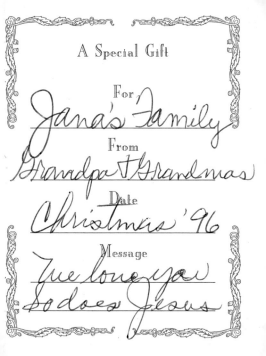

A Special Gift

For

Jana's Family

From

Grandpa & Grandmas

Date

Christmas '96

Message

We love you
So does Jesus

Welcome every stumbling
block and every torn and
jagged rock,
For each one is a stepping-stone
To God, who wants you
for His own.

*He drew me up from the
desolate pit, out of the miry bog,
and set my feet upon a rock,
making my steps secure.*

Psalm 40:2

Today view your problems
with a spiritual perspective. See
each difficulty as a lesson in
problem solving and endurance.

Wait with a heart that is patient
For the goodness of
God to prevail,
For never do our prayers
go unanswered
And His mercy and love
never fail.

*Rest in the Lord and wait
patiently for Him.*

Psalm 37:7 NAS

Today call to Him. Display
your patience and be a
peacemaker.

Time is not measured
By the years that you live,
But by the deeds that you do
And the joy that you give.

*Those who devise good meet
loyalty and faithfulness.*
Proverbs 14:22

Today recognize the importance
of doing an act of kindness. One
small deed accomplished is
better than a hundred
unfulfilled promises.

"Thou wilt keep him in
perfect peace
Whose mind is stayed
on Thee …"
And, God, if anyone needs
peace it certainly is me!

*A man's spirit will endure
sickness; but a broken spirit
who can bear?*

Proverbs 18:14

Today avoid being judgmental.
Eliminate resentment and
bitterness, and your personal
peace will increase.

There's something we should not forget – that people we've known or heard of or met by indirection have a big part in molding the thoughts of the mind and the heart.

A man's heart deviseth his way: but the Lord directeth his steps.

Proverbs 16:9 KJV

Today display enthusiasm, confidence, commitment, and determination. Your zeal for living and your love of God could be contagious.

Take the Saviour's loving hand
And do not try to understand,
Just let Him lead you
where He will,
Through pastures green, by
waters still.

*Know that the Lord is God! It is
he that made us, and we are his;
we are his people, and the sheep
of his pasture.*

Psalm 100:3

Today follow the Shepherd.
Encourage the sheep who have
strayed to return to the fold.

Take a cup of kindness,
Mix it well with love,
Add a lot of patience
And faith in God above.

*Be patient and you will finally
win, for a soft tongue can
break hard bones.*
Proverbs 25:15 TLB

Today blend kindness, love,
and patience. Sift in a generous
amount of faith. You'll have a
no-fail recipe for life.

Some folks grow older with
birthdays, it's true, but others
grow nicer as years
widen their view.
No one will notice a few little
wrinkles when a kind, loving
heart fills the eyes
full of twinkles.

*Grandchildren are the crown
of the aged ...*

Proverbs 17:6

Today fill an emptiness in
someone's life. Irrespective of
age, you can add happiness and
eliminate loneliness in another
person's day.

Prayer is so often just
words unspoken,
Whispered in tears by a heart
that is broken …
For God is already deeply aware
Of the burdens we find too
heavy to bear.

I am utterly spent and crushed;
I groan because of the tumult
of my heart.

Psalm 38:8

Today exemplify tolerance and
forgiveness. Promote
reconciliation with those who
have offended you.

Only with the help of God
Can we meet the vast
unknown …
Even the strongest of us cannot
Do the job alone!

Hasten, O God, to save me; O
Lord, come quickly to help me.

Psalm 70:1 NIV

Today flex your spiritual
muscles. Warm up, tone, and
exercise your values and ideals.

The more you do unselfishly,
The more you live abundantly
The more of everything
you share,
The more you'll always have
to spare.

*O Lord, my heart is not lifted
up, my eyes are not raised too
high; I do not occupy myself
with things too great and too
marvelous for me.*

Psalm 131:1

Today contemplate the
magnitude of tasks that can be
accomplished if there is no
concern with receiving praise
or credit.

May the people of all nations
At last become aware
That God will solve the people's
problems
Through faith and hope and
prayer!

*I am thy servant; give me
understanding, that I may know
thy testimonies!*

Psalm 119:125

Today take pride in your
country and in those who
defend it.

The love you give to others
Is returned to you by the Lord,
And the love of God
Is your soul's rich reward.

*One man is lavish yet grows still
richer; another is too sparing,
yet is the poorer.*

Proverbs 11:24 NAB

Today heal wounds. Healing
has a domino effect.

Let nothing sway you
Or turn you away
From God's old commandments
– they are still new today.

*Praise the Lord. Blessed is the
man who fears the Lord, who
greatly delights in his
commandments!*

Psalm 112:1

Today live by God's standards,
not the world's standards.

It's by completing what God
gives us to do
That we find real contentment
and happiness, too.

Requite them according to their
work, and according to the evil
of their deeds; requite them
according to the work of their
hands; render them their
due reward.

Psalm 28:4

Today eliminate
procrastination. Complete the
task before you.

Instead of just idle supposing
Step forward to meet each new
day, secure in the knowledge
God's near you, to lead you each
step of the way.

*When you walk, your steps will
not be hampered; when you run,
you will not stumble.*

Proverbs 4:12 NIV

Today accept the challenge that
rests in the dawning of each new
day. Appreciate God's presence
and guidance. He will protect
you if you stumble.

If you would find the Saviour,
No need to search afar –
For God is all around you,
No matter where you are!

*Thou dost beset me behind and
before, and layest thy hand
upon me.*
Psalm 139:5

Today be alert to God's
presence – in yourself, in others,
in nature.

I meet God in the morning
And go with Him through the
day, then in the stillness of the
night before sleep comes, I pray.

*I rise before dawn and cry for
help; I wait for Thy words.
My eyes anticipate the night
watches, that I may meditate
on Thy word.*
Psalm 119: 147, 148 NAS

Today, whatever the hour,
wherever the place, assemble
your thoughts and prayers and
with a thankful heart present
them to God.

I pray that God will just take over all the problems I couldn't solve, and I'm ready for tomorrow with all my cares dissolved.

But I will sing of thy might; I will sing aloud of thy steadfast love in the morning. For thou hast been to me a fortress and a refuge in the day of my distress.

Psalm 59:16

Today release your worries into God's hands. Solutions are His speciality.

The house of prayer is no
farther away
Than the quiet spot where you
kneel and pray,
For the heart is a temple when
God is there
As you place yourself in His
loving care.

*I bow down toward thy holy
temple and give thanks to thy
name for thy steadfast love and
thy faithfulness ...*
Psalm 138:2

Today remember that any place
is a good place to pray and
thank God.

Growing older only means
The spirit grows serene,
And we behold things
with our souls
That our eyes have never seen.

*So even to old age and grey
hairs, O God, do not forsake me,
till I proclaim thy might to all
the generations to come.*

Psalm 71:18

Today appreciate those who are
older. Value their advice. Seek
their companionship.

The golden chain of friendship
Is a strong and blessed tie,
Binding kindred hearts together
As the years go passing by.

*Do good, O Lord, unto those
that be good, and to them that
are upright in their hearts.*
Psalm 125:4 KJV

Today polish your chain of
friendship. Keep it tarnish-free.

God is the master builder,
His plans are perfect and true,
And when He sends you sorrow,
It's part of His plan for you.

For thou, O God, hast tested us;
thou hast tried us as silver
is tried.

Psalm 66:10

Today sculpt and work on your
life – for you are creating a
masterpiece – a work of art in
partnership with God.

God did not promise sun without rain, light without darkness or joy without pain – He only promised us strength for the day when the darkness comes and we lose our way.

If I say, "Let only darkness cover me, and the light about me be night," even the darkness is not dark to thee, the night is bright as the day; for darkness is as light with thee.

Psalm 139:11, 12

Today generate understanding and radiate love. Try turning the light on in the life of another individual.

Father, make us kind and wise
So we may always recognise
The blessings that are ours to take
And the friendships that are ours
to make.

*There are "friends" who
pretend to be friends, but there
is a friend who sticks closer
than a brother.*

Proverbs 18:24 TLB

Today restore any broken
relationship. Maintain and
support your friendships. A
friend is a gift from God.

A mother's love is something
That no one can explain,
It is made of deep devotion
And of sacrifice and pain.

*Her children rise up and call
her blessed; her husband also,
and he praises her.*

Proverbs 31:28

Today honour and remember
your mother in an appropriate
manner – a visit, a prayer,
a message.

Everything is by comparison,
Both the bitter and the sweet,
And it takes a bit of
both of them
To make our lives complete.

He who is full loathes honey, but
to the hungry even what is bitter
tastes sweet.

Proverbs 27:7 NIV

Today maintain an attitude of
thanksgiving. Be thankful for all
events in your life: sorrows and
joys, failures and successes, the
valleys and the mountains.

Discipline in daily duty
Will shape your life for deeper
beauty,
And as you grow in strength and
grace,
The more clearly you can see
God's face.

May God be gracious to us and
bless us and make his face to
shine upon us.
Psalm 67:1

Today strict training and self-
control will result in an increase
of mercy and effective power.

All things work together
To complete the master plan,
And God up in heaven
Can see what's best for man.

Yet God my King is from of old,
working salvation in the midst of
the earth.

Psalm 74:12

Today cooperate with God,
dedicate and consecrate your
efforts to Him, and you'll be
pleasantly surprised by the
Master of the Universe.

Whenever we are troubled
And life has lost its song,
It's God testing us with burdens
Just to make our spirit strong!

*This is my comfort in my
affliction that thy promise
gives me life.*
Psalm 119:50

Today face your challenges
with determination and
resiliency.

Whatever we ask for
Falls short of God's giving,
For His greatness exceeds
Every facet of living.

*Great is the Lord, and greatly to
be praised, and his greatness is
unsearchable.*

Psalm 145:3

Today be liberal in your praise
of and your gratitude to God.
The degree of His generosity is
beyond compare and the scope
of His giving is unfathomable.

We rob our lives much more than we know when we fail to respond or in any way show our thanks for the blessings that are daily ours – the warmth of the sun, the fragrance of flowers.

All Thy works shall give thanks to Thee … They shall speak of the glory of Thy kingdom, and talk of Thy power …

Psalm 145:10-12 NAS

Today cultivate an appreciation for the beauty in nature.

A warm, ready smile or a kind,
thoughtful deed or a hand
Outstretched in an hour of need
Can change our outlook and
make the world bright
Where a minute before just
nothing seemed right.

*A brother helped is like a strong
city, but quarreling is like the
bars of a castle.*

Proverbs 18:19

Today bring a brilliance to the
world around you with a smile
and an act of kindness.

To be peaceful, I must be kind
For peace can't exist in a hate-
torn mind,
So to have peace I must
always show
Love to all people I meet,
see, or know.

*... he who respects the
commandment will be rewarded*
Proverbs 13:13

Today erase all signs of hatred
– let love and peace prevail.

Teach me to be patient
In everything I do,
Content to trust Your wisdom
And to follow after You.

*Do not fret because of evil men
or be envious of the wicked, for
the evil man has no future hope,
and the lamp of the wicked will
be snuffed out.*

Proverbs 24:19, 20 NIV

Today practice patience.
Practice makes perfect.

Take ample time
For heartfelt conversation,
Establish with our Father
An unbreakable relation.

A word fitly spoken is like
apples of gold in pictures
of silver.
Proverbs 25:11 KJV

Today converse with God
morning, noon, and night.

Someday may man realise
That all the earth,
the seas, and skies
Belong to God who made us all,
The rich, the poor
the great, the small!

*My mouth is filled with thy
praise, and with thy glory
all the day.*

Psalm 71:8

Today feel the awe and the
wonder of God's creation.

Prayers are not meant
for obtaining
What we selfishly wish
to acquire,
For God in His wisdom refuses
The things that we
wrongly desire.

*I have remembered Thine
ordinances from of old, O Lord,
and comfort myself.*

Psalm 119:52 NAS

Today infuse your prayers with
praise and thanksgiving to God.

Not money or material things,
But understanding and
the joy that it brings
Can change this old world
and its selfish ways
And put goodness and mercy
back into our days.

By wisdom a house is built, and
by understanding it is
established ...
Proverbs 24:3, 4

Today give someone a piece of
your time, wrapped with
understanding and compassion.

Tender little memories
Of some word or deed
Give us strength and courage
When we are in need.

*For the righteous will never
be moved; he will be
remembered forever.*

Psalm 112:6

Today reflect upon a past
kindness and the strength it
afforded both the giver and
the receiver.

The more we endure
With patience and grace,
The stronger we grow
And the more we can face.

*The Lord is the strength of his
people, the saving refuge
of his anointed.*

Psalm 28.8 NAB

Today grow stronger as you
adopt the policy of patiently
addressing the problems that
confront you.

Kindness is a virtue
Given by the Lord,
It pays dividends in happiness
And joy is its reward.

*A wicked man earns deceptive
wages, but one who sows
righteousness gets a
sure reward.*

Proverbs 11:18

Today add kindness to
someone else's life and your
own happiness will be
multiplied.

The joy of enjoying
And the fullness of living
Are found in the heart
That is filled with thanksgiving.

Deceit fills hearts that are
plotting for evil; joy fills hearts
that are planning for good!
Proverbs 12:20 *TLB*

Today let your heart overflow
with gratitude and your joy
will increase.

It's a wonderful world and it
always will be
If we open our eyes and see
The wonderful things man is
capable of
When he opens his heart to God
and His love.

*God looks down from heaven
upon the sons of men to see if
there are any that are wise, that
seek after God.*

Psalm 53:2

Today unlock the chambers of
your heart and ask God to enter
in. His presence will transfuse
your life.

In the beauty of a snowflake
Falling softly on the land
Is the mystery and miracle
Of God's great, creative hand!

*Praise the Lord from the earth
… fire and hail, snow and
clouds; stormy wind fulfilling
His word.*

Psalm 148:7, 8 NAS

Today observe the loveliness of
a wintry scene. Each snowflake,
like each human being, is
special and has its own
individual characteristics.

I'm way down here!
You're way up there!
Are You sure You can hear
My faint, faltering prayer?

*Hear my prayer, O Lord, and
give ear to my cry; hold not thy
peace at my tears! For I am thy
passing guest, a sojourner, like
all my fathers.*

Psalm 39:12

Today call to God. He hears
you always and at all times.

I give to You my thanks
And my heart kneels to pray –
God keep me and guide me
And go with me today.

*Thou dost guide me with thy
counsel, and afterward thou wilt
receive me to glory.*

Psalm 73:24

Today ask God to guide, guard,
and go with you.

Help us to remember
That the key to life and living
Is to make each prayer a
prayer of thanks
And every day "Thanksgiving."

*I will praise the name of God
with a song, and will magnify
him with thanksgiving.*

Psalm 69:30 KJV

Today be thankful for your
blessings and share with those
not so well-blessed. Be grateful
for your talents. Use some
degree of those talents to help
those in need.

God's kindness is ever
around you,
Always ready to freely impart
Strength to your faltering spirit,
Cheer to your lonely heart.

*When the cares of my heart
are many, thy consolations
cheer my soul.*

Psalm 94:19

Today express your thanks to
Jesus for touching your life.

God's heavens are dotted with
uncounted jewels,
For joy without measure is one
of God's rules.
His hand is so generous, His
heart is so great,
He comes not too soon, and He
comes not too late.

*In the beginning you laid the
foundations of the earth, and the
heavens are the work of
your hands.*
Psalm 102:25 NIV

Today realise that God needs no
alarm clocks, wristwatches, or
timers.

God, I know that I love You,
And I know without doubt
That Your goodness and mercy
Never run out.

Surely goodness and mercy shall
follow me all the days
of my life …
Psalm 23:6

Today count the many ways
that you observe God's
goodness and mercy.

"The earth is the Lord's
And the fullness thereof" –
It speaks of His greatness,
It sings of His love.

*The heavens are yours, the
world, everything – for you
created them all.*

Psalm 89:11 TLB

Today reflect on the greatness
of our Creator as you listen to
the earth's melody.

Do you pause in meditation
Upon life's thoroughfare,
And offer up thanksgiving –
Or say a word of prayer?

*Then my tongue shall tell of thy
righteousness and of thy praise
all the day long.*

Psalm 35:28

Today devote a portion of your
day to reflecting on God's role
in your life and your role in
God's plan.

Do justice, love kindness, walk
humbly with God –
With these three things as your
rule and your rod
All things worth having are
yours to achieve
If you follow God's words and
have faith to believe!

*He loves righteousness and
justice; the earth is full of the
loving kindness of the Lord.*

Psalm 33:5 NAS

Today apply Christ's
principles.

An unlit candle gives no light,
Only when burning,
is it shining bright,
And if life is empty,
dull and dark,
It's doing things for others that
gives the needed spark.

Yea, thou dost light my lamp;
the Lord my God lightens
my darkness.
Psalm 18:28

Today light up someone's life
and you'll generate happiness
for yourself.

Remember God loves you
And wants to protect you,
So seek that small haven
And be guided by prayer
To that place of protection
Within God's loving care.

Every word of God proves true.
He defends all who come to
him for protection
Proverbs 30:5 TLB

Today seek safety and security
in God's everlasting arms.

It doesn't matter where we pray
If we honestly mean
the words we say,
For God is always
listening to hear
The prayers that are made by a
heart that's sincere.

*In the day of my trouble I call on
thee, for thou dost answer me.*

Psalm 86:7

Today pray with sincerity
and simplicity.

If we put our problems in
God's hand,
There is nothing we
need understand.
It is enough to just believe
That what we need
we will receive.

*If I take the wings of the
morning, and dwell in the
uttermost parts of the sea; even
there shall thy hand lead me,
and thy right hand
shall hold me.*

Psalm 139:9, 10 KJV

Today let go and let God help
solve your dilemma.

All I need do
Is to silently pray –
"God, help me and guide me
And go with me today."

Good and upright is the Lord;
therefore he instructs sinners in
his ways. He guides the humble
in what is right and teaches
them his way.

Psalm 25:8, 9 NIV

Today keep God as your
constant companion.

With our hands we give gifts
that money can buy, diamonds
that sparkle like stars in the sky,
But only the heart can give
away the gift of peace and
a perfect day.

*May the Lord give strength to
his people! May the Lord bless
his people with peace!*

Psalm 29:11

Today ask yourself, "If I were
gift wrapped as a package for
Jesus, would He be pleased to
receive me?

Whenever you are hurried
And must leave
something undone
Be sure it's not
your prayer to God
At dawn or setting sun.

*It is good to give thanks to the
LORD, to sing praise to your
name, Most High, to proclaim
your kindness at dawn and your
faithfulness throughout
the night.*

Psalm 92: 1, 2 NAB

Today and every day make
time to pray.

What must I do to insure peace
of mind?
Is the answer I'm seeking, too
hard to find?
How can I know what God
wants me to be?
How can I tell what's
expected of me?

*Many are the plans in the mind
of a man, but it is the purpose of
the Lord that will be established.*

Proverbs 19:21

Persevere in accomplishing
that which God has in mind for
you to do.

What is love? No words
can define it.
It's something so great, only
God could design it.
Yes, love is beyond what man
can define,
For love is immortal and God's
gift is divine.

*Praise him who alone does
mighty miracles, for his loving
kindness continues forever.*

Psalm 136:4 TLB

Today surprise someone with a
phone call or a joyous greeting.
Permit God's love to overflow
through you and your actions.

Teach me sweet forbearance
When things do not go right,
So I remain unruffled
When others grow uptight.

*If you faint in the day of
adversity, your strength is small.*
Proverbs 24:10

Today demonstrate forbearance
in your language, your actions,
and your reactions. A calm, well
thought out response has a
soothing effect on others.

Teach me how to quiet
My racing, rising heart,
So I may hear the answer
You are trying to impart.

My son, give me your heart and
let your eyes keep to my ways.
Proverbs 23:26 NIV

Today calm someone else's
fears and maintain a serenity of
your own.

The silent stars in timeless skies,
The wonderment in
children's eyes,
A rosebud in a slender vase
Are all reflections of God's face.

*Hear, O Lord, when I cry aloud,
be gracious to me and answer
me! Thou hast said, "Seek
ye my face." My heart says to
thee. "Thy face, Lord, do I
seek." Hide not thy
face from me.*

Psalm 27:7-9

Today observe your
surroundings with a spiritual
vision. You'll locate God in
places never before imagined.

Prayers are the stairs
that lead to God,
And there's joy every step
of the way
When we make our
pilgrimage to Him
With love in our hearts
each day.

*The steps of a good man are
ordered by the Lord: and he
delighteth in his way.*

Psalm 37:23 KJV

Today revive your weary heart
with prayer as you climb closer
to God.

Only by the grace of God
Can we gain self-control,
And only meditative thoughts
Can restore our peace of soul.

*In peace I will both lie down
and sleep; for thou alone, O
Lord, makest me dwell in safety.*
Psalm 4:8

Today if you have a difference
of opinion with someone,
disagree but don't be
disagreeable.

Memories to treasure
Are made of Christmas Day,
Made of family gatherings
And children as they play.

*Your wife shall be like a fruitful
vine, within your house, your
children like olive plants around
your table.*

Psalm 128:3 NAS

Today treasure remembrances
of the past and joys of the
present by sharing your love
with family members, children,
grandchildren, relatives
or friends.

May the holy remembrance
Of the first Christmas Day
Be our reassurance
Christ is not far away.

*Upon thee was I cast from my
birth, and since my mother bore
me thou hast been my God.*

Psalm 22:10

Today live your life in such a
manner that others can look for
and recognize Jesus within you.

May every heart and
every home
Continue through the year
To feel the warmth and wonder
Of this season of good cheer.

Lord, when doubts fill my mind,
when my heart is in turmoil,
quiet me and give me renewed
hope and cheer.

Psalm 94:19 TLB

Today pledge to maintain all
year the warmth of love and
cordiality generated by this
Christmas season.

Make us aware
That the Christmas story
Is everyone's promise
Of eternal glory.

*Not to us, O Lord, not to us, but
to thy name give glory, for the
sake of thy steadfast love and
thy faithfulness!*

Psalm 115:1

Today send some of your own
love into the world. You don't
have to buy it, box it, wrap it, tie
it – just give love away.

In counting our blessings,
We find when we're through
We've no reason at all
To complain or be blue.

*A faithful man shall abound
with blessings ...*
Proverbs 28:20 KJV

Today count your loved ones as
your top priority and blessing. It
is also important to be
remembered by your loved ones.
For which reason, characteristic,
personality trait, or act of
kindness do you wish to be
remembered? Think about it.
Work on it.

If we lived Christmas each day
as we should,
And made it our aim
to always do good,
We'd find the lost key to
meaningful living
That comes not from getting,
but from unselfish giving.

He is ever giving liberally and
lending, and his children
become a blessing.

Psalm 37:26

Today live by the principle,
"It's far more blessed to give
than to receive."

Just like the seasons that come
and go
When the flowers of spring lay
buried in snow,
God sends to the heart in its
winter of sadness
A springtime awakening of new
hope and gladness.

*And now, Lord, for what do I
wait? My hope is in thee.*

Psalm 39:7

Today clear away the icy
feelings of despair and uncover
the gladness buried in
your heart.

It matters not who or
what you are,
All men can behold the
Christmas Star.
For the Star that shone is
shining still
In the hearts of men of peace
and goodwill.

*Restore to me the joy of thy
salvation, and uphold me with a
willing spirit.*
Psalm 51:12

Today trim your life with an
inner beauty. The Star shines for
one and all.

In the glad tidings
Of the first Christmas night,
God showed us
The way and the truth
and the light.

O send out Thy light and Thy
truth, let them lead me; let them
bring me to Thy holy hill, and to
Thy dwelling places.

Psalm 43:3 NAS

Today appreciate the
magnificent and generous gift of
God's love.

Humbly, I realize that He who
made the sea and skies
And holds the whole world in
His hand also has my small soul
in His command.

*The law of the Lord is perfect,
reviving the soul ... the
commandment of the Lord is
pure, enlightening the eyes.*

Psalm 19:7, 8

Today acknowledge the
vastness and also the gentleness
of God's power. The depths,
breadths, lengths, and widths of
the universe are God's creations
and the control rests in His hands.

God, make us aware
that in Thy name
The Holy Christ Child
humbly came
To live on earth and
leave behind
New faith and hope for all
mankind.

I wait for the Lord, my soul
waits, and in his word
I put my hope.

Psalm 130:5 NIV

Today radiate with the glow of
Christmas time. Jesus came to
earth as a baby. Look for the
innocence, purity, goodness, and
love in those around you.

The gifts that we give
have no purpose
Unless God is part of the giving,
And unless we make
Christmas a pattern
To be followed in
everyday living.

*A man's gift makes room for
him and brings him before
great men.*

Proverbs 18:16

Today share a gift with your
feathered, flying friends. The
birds will appreciate water, suet,
and seed. God made all
creatures.

Christmas to me
Is a gift from above –
A gift of salvation
Born of God's love.

Love and faithfulness meet together; righteousness and peace kiss each other.

Psalm 85:10 NIV

Today decorate your life with glad tidings, cheer, and an inner glow that develops through loving Jesus and living in a manner pleasing to Him.

Christmas is more than a day
at the end of the year,
More than a season of joy and
good cheer,
Christmas is really God's
pattern for living
To be followed all year by
unselfish giving.

*I give thee thanks, O Lord, with
my whole heart ... for thou hast
exalted above everything thy
name and thy word.*

Psalm 138:1, 2

Today accept the treasured gift
from God called peace!

By completing what God
Gives us to do,
We find real contentment
And happiness, too.

*God blesses those who obey
him; happy the man who puts
his trust in the Lord.*

Proverbs 16:20 TLB

Today awaken the laughter in
your heart and relax a little in
these hectic days.

Miracles are marvels
That defy all explanation
And Christmas is a miracle,
Not just a celebration.

*I will give to the Lord the thanks
due to his righteousness, and I
will sing praise to the name of
the Lord, the Most High.*

Psalm 7:17

Today marvel at the
significance and meaning of the
miracle of Christmas.

By keeping Christ in Christmas
We are helping to fulfill
The glad tidings of the angels –
"Peace on earth and to
men, goodwill."

*Let me hear what God the Lord
will speak, for he will speak
peace to his people, to his
saints, to those who turn to him
in their hearts.*

Psalm 85:8

Today respond to someone
else's anger with gentleness on
your part. Anger begets anger so
put a halt to the cycle. Greater
strength is shown by those who
choose kindness as a reaction.

A baby is a gift of life
Born of the wonder of love –
A little bit of eternity,
Sent from the Father above.

*Behold, [children] are a gift
from the Lord: the fruit of the
womb is a reward.*

Psalm 127:3 NAB

Today consider the glory, the
wonder, and the beauty involved
in the gift of life.

Be not disheartened by troubles, for trials are the building blocks on which to erect a fortress of faith Secure on God's ageless rocks.

In thee, O Lord, do I take refuge; let me never be put to shame! ... Be thou to me a rock of refuge, a strong fortress, to save me, for thou art my rock and my fortress.

Psalm 71:1, 3

Display courage and inner fortitude when misfortunes befall you. Be assured God is ever near.

At this holy season
Give us quietness of mind,
Teach us to be patient
And help us to be kind.

*Let them give thanks to the Lord
for His loving kindness, and for
His wonders to the sons of men!*

Psalm 107:31 NAS

Today eliminate condemnation
and display compassion.
Kindness is appreciated now
and anytime of the year.

After the night, the morning,
Bidding all darkness cease,
After life's cares and sorrows,
The comfort and
sweetness of peace.

*O Lord, my God, I call for help
by day; I cry out in the night
before thee.*
Psalm 88:1

Today practice stability and
dependability. They are just as
necessary in life as having
an ability.

Above the noise and laughter
That is empty, cruel, and loud,
Do you listen for
the voice of God
In the restless, surging crowd?

Thy steadfast love, O Lord,
extends to the heavens, thy
faithfulness to the clouds.
Psalm 36:5

Today observe the relationship
of happiness and helpfulness:
the extent of your happiness is
commensurate with the degree
of your helpfulness to others.

After the night, the morning,
Bidding all darkness cease,
After life's cares and sorrows,
The comfort and
sweetness of peace.

O Lord, my God, I call for help
by day; I cry out in the night
before thee.
Psalm 88:1

Today practice stability and
dependability. They are just as
necessary in life as having
an ability.

Above the noise and laughter
That is empty, cruel, and loud,
Do you listen for
the voice of God
In the restless, surging crowd?

Thy steadfast love, O Lord,
extends to the heavens, thy
faithfulness to the clouds.

Psalm 36:5

Today observe the relationship
of happiness and helpfulness:
the extent of your happiness is
commensurate with the degree
of your helpfulness to others.